T0209403

THE
UNCONSTITUTIONAL
and
UNWRITTEN LAWS
of
CRIME

MALEKH SALTERS

iUniverse

THE UNCONSTITUTIONAL AND UNWRITTEN LAWS OF CRIME

Power In Numbers Publishing LLC
Orginal Editor: Sahran Odom

iUniverse books may be ordered through booksellers or by contacting:

iUniverse
1663 Liberty Drive
Bloomington, IN 47403
www.iuniverse.com
844-349-9409

ISBN: 978-1-6632-5057-5 (sc)
ISBN: 978-1-6632-5059-9 (e)

Library of Congress Control Number: 2023902365

Print information available on the last page.

iUniverse rev. date: 05/31/2023

DEDICATION

Father: Gavriel Ori-Ben Judah

Mother: Denise Salters(Rest In Peace)

Sister: Deshaun Laurel Bailey

Sister-In-Law: Lisa Salters

Brother: Maliek Salters

Brother: Bruce Hough

Brother-In-Law(s): Charles Bailey Jr., Thomas Hines Sr., and Kareem Hines

Significant other: Rashonda Moye

Uncle(s): Steven Simpkins(Rest In Peace), Leon Simpkins, Timothy Simpkiins, Pete Hillary, Alfred Cook, William Odom and Larry Smith

Aunt(s): Loustine Green, Betty Ann Daise, Maxine Harley(Rest In Peace), Margie Hillary, Eleanor Cook, Lillian Odom,Nanette Simpkins and Janice Simpkins-Smith

Cousin(s): Shyvron Simpkins, Century Harley III(Rest In Peace), Thalia C. Gaymon, Christina Simpkins, Steven Simpkins Jr.,, Tiara Simpkins, Brittany Simpkins, James Smith, Syneta Valentine, Antawn Hilllary, Cory Hillary, Aramis Hillary, Courtney Simpkins, Leon Benjamin Simpkins, Malcolm Cook,

Aaron Cook, Jacob Cook, Candice Simpkins, Michael Thomas, Lovelle Salters, Paulette Diase, Toby Daise, Anita Daise O'Dell Daise, Anthony Daise, Kim Daise, Nechemiah Dunbar, Kimberly Dunbar, Mendya Griffin and Darryl "Didum" Griffin

Nephew(s): Charles Bailey III, Kyntel Kyle Thomas Hines, Manny Parker, Hasan Hamilton, Amari Salters, Malik Hough, Elijah Hough

Niece(s): Q'Yara Thompasionas, Tytiana Hines, Kyana HInes, Nijala S. Bledsoe, Nyima Hough, GraceLynn Laurel Hines

Brotherly: Jamile Davis(Rest In Peace), Timothy Moses Jr.,, Abdul Muqit, Malcolm Glass, John Troy Brewster, Sean Brewster, Dehane Davis, Andre Dicks, Brian Dick, Brandon Anderson, Darryl Mac, Dale Parker, Tone Zeigler, Justin O'Jeda, Harry Cheatman, Javar Cheatman, Tone Davis, Leonard Owens, Dwight Bent(Rest In Peace), Quentin Gamble(Rest In Peace), Khalid Huggins, Wendy Germain, Sean Ramlakhan, Ian Hunte, Michael Rock, Tristan Verette, Dominique Edouarzin, Roland Chassagne Desmond Pras and Antawn Prescott

Sisterly: Bettina Pendleton, Michelle Rivera, Natasha Haynes, Antoinette Henry, Jade Verette, Kay Wallijee, Karen Wynn, Gina Arezza and Janae

Barcelona Bar: Jason Sturm, Michael Knight, Chris Ryan, John Policino, Brian Prince, Matthew Clifford, Giovanni Gonzalez, Griogio Spano, Ryan, Darryl B., Amber Levine, Brian Dalton, Lue

Rios-Gonzalez, Rodney Epps, Mike Mike Epps, Adam Liscombe, Brookes Broughton, Adam Bohanon, Greg Nice, Adam Santiago, Eric Schmidt, Eric Young, Anthony Fufaro, Kacper Grochowalski, Kenzo Capulong, Gloria Gutierrez, Randy Dorleans, Diana Wallwork, Ethan Wolfe and Eddie Mendez

McHales Bar and Grill: Paul Downey, Chef Nick Rizzo, Bethany Edlund-Downey, Christopher Downey, Alberto Baltazar, Neill O'Reilly, Cabs D. Nunez, Melina Kiely, Molly Long, Brighid Mallon, Kieran O'Sullivan, Robin Higginbotham, Rick Wesley, Irene Thorton, Nick Pearson, Sadie Seekamp, Catherine Torres, Matthew Juarez Adrian Juarez, Flor Gonzalez, Jeber Coxolca, Zoe McIntyre Gonzalez, Nora Nolan, J.J. Hoss, Paul Corbett and Ana Valdes

Patron(s): John Gordan, Colby Foytik, Tommy Schultz, Michael Balderrama, Brian Hayes, Jason Coppola, Sean Cummisky, Michael Hallian, Paul Descazi, Ed Lewis, Justin Guifoyle, Damon Yuhasz, Mark Johannes, Eric and Anisa Gilley, Nicole Garcia, Bianca DiSarro, Cynthia Cologne, Nick Thomas, Darryl and Amanda Brown

Arts and Crafts Beer Parlor: Robert LaFrance, Richard LaFrance, Phil Cunningham, Colin Gallagher, Holly Gallagher, Jonathan Simmons, Jeff Dattilo and John Moores

Shoutouts: Manouchka "Onyx" McKissick and Madeline Pendleton-Lewis

Special Thanks: Manouchka "Onyx" Mckissick, Rufaro Nyangoni, Madeline Pendleton-Lewis and Francesca "Cess" Tessier

CONTENTS

PREFACE

This book was created for the sole purpose of educating proprietors, partners, and organizations operating in a career criminal enterprise. I have written guidelines to help increase success and longevity. There are those who may have had other options but deemed crime the most beneficial path for whatever reason. Others may believe they aren't skilled at anything else because of certain factors, such as lack of parenting and poverty, limiting their options. I could give you a thousand reasons—or some would say excuses—why some would choose this path, but the fact remains that it was chosen. Not all criminal participants are troublesome; they just haven't discovered their self-worth yet.

Countless times, I have witnessed the tragedy of how a life of crime can crush the criminal participant, such as the number of years lost to incarceration, physical scarring for life from violence, assassination attempts, constantly being on the run, hiding out, and losing their identity. Unfortunately a life of crime only has a negative outcome. I have examined most angles and added up the variables in this equation to create the most desirable outcome. I believe that with the correct tools and strategy applied, there is a right way to do the wrong thing. My intention is to help minimize the ills that come with a criminal lifestyle; protect the integrity of the business; and self-preserve the criminal participant, which I call the "under accomplished."

This particular group of people know how to accomplish things in life, but can't identify their ultimate goal or purpose. For those who believe this is their destiny, love the lifestyle, or are just addicted to the rush, I can guarantee a loss of freedom, demise, or endangerment of loved ones. Take this book, and apply it to your criminal lifestyle. Receive what you need from it. Knowing when to quit is crucial. Not doing so will make all the information you've acquired pointless in the end. If you don't have an exit plan to this lifestyle, you will be chasing a death wish. Anyone who wishes to play it out to the end is a fool. It is not considered quitting if you are already ahead.

There have been books on the good, the bad, and the ugly. Now it's time for the misunderstood. Welcome *to The Unconstitutional and Unwritten Laws of Crime*, a written tutorial for a lifestyle that has no scriptures, but consider this your bible.

Opportunity versus Idealism

Exasperated with being victimized by society, you awaken, arise, and plant your feet with the intention of eradicating the awful life patterns experienced by choosing crime. There are only two ways to enter the world of crime: a given opportunity or idealism. Opportunity isn't the better of the two, but if you can't tolerate your lifestyle for another second, just remember that you are going into an operation half-cocked.

Your control is limited because you don't have ownership, which means you are expendable and at their disposal any time they choose. When you enter someone else's world, beware. You may not know what forces lurk in the dark. How can you know unless you are aware of the mastermind's misfortune? Apply Murphy's Law, which states, "What can go wrong, will go wrong."

The hidden agenda of the mastermind is that he or she will always try to sell how great the operation and business is. They will not offer you the opportunity for your benefit but for their own. You have a skill or habit that the mastermind can exploit. This makes you momentarily useful if you can't pass up the opportunity, and they deem you useful. Use it to build capital to start your own operation, illegally or legally—it's your choice.

Idealism should be the favorable of the two, if you have any brain power. You envisioned the ideal, which demonstrated leadership. Now that you have an idea, the next thing to do is create it. Start with the idea. Venture outside the box, and build everything around the idea. Don't do anything extra or unnecessary; it will only complicate the plan. Once that's complete, it's time to put the plan into action. In order to do so, you must have tunnel vision, which is the ability to see a plan through, from start to finish, without distractions. To successfully implement this process, you must have a clear mind and deep concentration to visualize your end goals. Consider these step-by-step procedures, and make chess moves. Think ahead. Your next move should always be your best move.

Now that you have created your blueprint, you can store it in your mental rolodex. Designs of this nature should never be written or recorded. If the complexity of the mental blueprint requires drawings to retrieve from memory, make sure they are destroyed immediately after or locked away with only your knowledge of their whereabouts. Now if you have the ability to operate without any partners, you are a pure genius, and I salute you. Otherwise, it's time to build your operation. It will consist of two components: team and tools.

The team should be handpicked from your immediate circle. This will eliminate the need for a background check. You should have known them for at least one decade, depending on your age. They should not be on parole; this helps deter law enforcement. You must know the characteristics of each member, as this will allow you to maneuver the team's future growth. Outsiders should not be permitted unless there are extreme circumstances, and they serve as a form of resolution to a problem. Each member of the team should have a particular set of skills that sets them apart from the rest of the crew. The team that stands by your side determines how successful your outcome will be.

The tools are devices that are set into place to create a successful outcome and minimize failure. Every tool keeps another tool in position. For example, let's say you are a supplier of illegal contraband. Your freedom and life will need to be protected to ensure preservation. Other entities will enter your realm to steal, neutralize, or eliminate your success, whether you are aware or not; therefore, you must seek measures to secure your safety. Lawyers, enforcers, accountants, store fronts, stash houses, surveillance cameras, untraceable or disposable cellular phones, and safes hidden in floors are all tools that have specific duties. If you notice room for error in your project, do not advance until the proper tool fills the slot.

Every tool is an important piece in completing the puzzle. You may have to replace or add new team members due to decay or growth. Socrates was a philosopher who believed that if matter was not decaying, it was growing, but there is a point at which the matter is stable. His understudy Plato had a theory of his own: two points existed, but there was no stability. Plato believed that stabilization didn't exist. It was a misconception of reality. For instance, let's take the anatomy of a teenager. There is no point where it is stable. It is growing, whether you realize it or not. If it is not growing in some form, it is most definitely decaying.

Here's another example: Your operation is growing, but you have a team member who is no longer happy participating in a criminal career. That person may be growing in other aspects of their life but decaying in the business. Inevitably they must be replaced because decay spreads throughout matter. That person's lack of interest or concern may affect the others. This is called transference of energy. Transference of energy can be negative or positive, depending on the source it is transferred from, so keep your circle tight and filled with positive energy.

Plato also had another theory called perception of reality, where a belief is powered by the brain, seen through the eyes, and signaled out into the universe, creating that belief. Transfer positive energy and channel your perception of reality by setting a common goal for all. Those two components will set your team in motion with purpose. A person without a plan is a person that plans to fail, and failure is not an option. Make sure the entire team has the same interests.

FEAR MET PARANOIA AND CREATED DEFENSES

Fear and paranoia are two emotional states that can turn into psychosis, but if properly controlled and calculated, they can provide countermeasures for would-be assaults. If applied correctly, they can become powerful components in deterring and detecting the unpredictable.

Fear is an unpleasant emotion caused by the belief that someone or something is dangerous and likely to cause pain or threat. It is an emotional response. Therefore, one has the choice to either indulge in it or not. Fear resonates from a person's early life experiences—most likely stemming from a terrifying incident that evolved into a phobia. Every human has a fear, but if there is one without fear, beware. If they are fearless, they have no boundaries and are highly unpredictable and dangerous. By acknowledging fear, one can make preparations to avoid confrontations.

Imagine you are a criminal, and your fear is prison. All your life, you've heard stories about people who were incarcerated. The images from war stories about riots, starvation, murder, and screams of men being sexually assaulted by other men are enough to fuel you to take every measure to avoid prison. If the time ever came for you to face prison, you would be more than prepared, because fear set this in motion in advance. There would be no need to strengthen yourself during incarceration; you would enter already physically fit and skilled in some form of martial arts. You would also be resourceful in arming yourself with surrounding materials, like modifying a toothbrush into a weapon. Fear can be a friend if you choose.

Paranoia is a mental condition characterized by delusions or unwarranted beliefs of persecution, jealousy, or exaggerated self-importance. A softer definition is the suspicion or distrust of people or their actions without evidence or justification. Paranoia is not always a psychotic feature of schizophrenia. A person's assumption might have some truth after all—just without supported evidence. If people assume you suffer from paranoia, they will say things like "get a grip" or "you need to relax," and they are somewhat correct. Empower the paranoia without allowing it to cause you to lose control. Completely dropping your guard and relaxing could be foolish. What if your theory of something or someone was correct, and you dropped your defenses? That play could render you helpless. Instead of overreacting or, even worse, attempting to deafen that constant ringing alarm of instinct, it should be put to use preparing measures in case you are correct.

Fear and paranoia together are a powerful combination of defense mechanisms. They also create an unexplained force and heightened sense of ability. The third eye is the ability to sense danger without seeing or hearing it, instead feeling it approach. The name came from people who said that this ability was like having an extra eye in the back of their heads. Use the alert signals as defense mechanisms to protocol security measures or ready yourself for immediate action.

The double check is a precaution where you reexamine a suspicion several times to clarify the feeling of paranoia. The double check is a great method of reassurance and should frequently be applied to your lifestyle, even if someone else thinks you are overacting. Always trust your instinct. That feeling in your gut just may be dead on, justifying your actions and benefiting you.

PURPOSE OF MONEY

Money is substantial to your survival in this lifestyle and will play a major role in your longevity, so nurture its growth. The accumulation of money is necessary and should not, by any means, be foolishly wasted. Money is useful in bargaining and gaining access through doors that you could not usually enter. It can aid and benefit you because of people's greed. They say everyone is expendable, and anyone can be bought. I peg myself on that being true, as money will purchase the things people crave most. Everyone has a price to some extent. So when money isn't the answer, use money to obtain the answer. Money will help you acquire the proper tools for your operations.

Hold onto money simply because you don't know what bumps lay ahead on your road to riches. There is no good in money, but you can do good things with it. This is why people say, "Make the money, but don't let the money make you." Money can alter one's perception of reality once they start acquiring a taste for the power it can bring. People tend to lose track of their original goals once they taste the power of having money. Don't get ahead of yourself because you have money, or you could find yourself staring down the barrel of some less-fortunate person's pistol.

Try to live a lifestyle of simplicity. The rules are simple, just like the name states. First, never live above your means. Second, don't buy just because you have money to spend. Third, a dollar saved is a dollar earned. Last, it's not how much you make but what you keep. Like Biggie said in "Ten Crack Commandments": "Follow these rules; you'll have mad bread to break up."

4

SUPREME CLIENTELE

Supreme clientele are those who become frequent associates of a particular business because of their vices, capabilities, and methods of business. This type of clientele ranges from buyer to seller, but they are rarities because of their ability to be reliable and predictable. It is best for this circle of clientele to be targeted, researched, and chosen without external influences, which will make for a smoother operation because of consistency.

Vouching for and influencing potential clientele to your operation should be impermissible. If things are slow, only you should require that your business provide vouchers to work with potential outbound clients. Cut them side deals, but absolutely do not meet. For potential clients, take a name, number, and the address of where you can find them. Do your homework first, before taking them aboard or bringing them in the circle. Observe them. Everybody has a weakness, so make sure to locate their poisons, which can be used as a means of control. The one downfall of supreme clientele is the relationships involved with family, friends, colleagues, and social acquaintances. They know you like you know them, so that makes you vulnerable.

When it comes to supreme clientele, the most important quality is trust. If that is broken, the relationship is compromised, and business is permanently tainted. Abort immediately. If your intuition kicks in and something seems strange or strays from the norm, that's your cue to abort.

5

PUBLIC EYE

This chapter will merely focus on you—the criminal—and how you present yourself in the eyes of the public. The underworld is a cesspool full of scum and a various assortment of unlikely characters such as cops, snitches, informants, witnesses, backstabbers, con artists, shysters, and robbers. From introduction to conclusion, my intention is simply to magnify your persona in the eyes of those you come in contact with, whether they be criminals or citizens. This approach is not to intimidate but to be used as a resolution in deterring the possible outcome of being a target or challenged. Most criminals believe that there is a sucker born every second, so the objective is to change how you are viewed in order to change that outcome, not by manipulating the public but by simply evolving your character. To become a force to be reckoned with, you will need each of these tools: appearance, conduct, book smarts, street smarts, and even southern hospitality. All are methods in becoming the sharpest tool in the toolbox.

Not every person will be convinced that your methods are practical or can bring a resolution. You could come in contact with a person of this nature, and the way you present yourself just might be the key to lowering the odds of you becoming their person of interest. Manners could be useful when talking with the wrong person. Considering your likeability. No one is invincible, so mind your manners, and talk to people how you wish to be talked to. Treat people how you would like to be treated. No one can constantly say and do whatever they want forever. It's only a matter of time before somebody steps up and attempts to put that person back in their proper place.

Now you can kill with kindness, but don't allow it to be mistaken for weakness. If this occurs, you will be forced to exploit your strengths to show their inferiority and keep your self-preservation intact, but even with this course of action, exercise diplomacy until you have no choice. Not every action can be undone once it has taken course.

The gray line between respect and fear is thin in regards to motives; they arise from different natures with opposite outcomes. Respect can be attained, and its reach is limitless. Respect is not often challenged but merely confronted as a means of resolving disagreements. Fear spreads quickly throughout the public and has psychological influence when used by means such as word of mouth and media. If you are not respected, make them fear you, but don't make a habit of incorporating fear into your daily agenda. It's only a matter of time before the fearful strike back, and you find yourself challenged by your public.

Your appearance doesn't have to be phenomenally upscaled, but at least being well groomed and having good hygiene is a must. Cleanliness is next to godliness. Don't slouch when you stand up, walk with your head down, or drag your feet when in motion. Those signs exhibit low self-esteem, which is a reflection of oneself, and are easily picked up by the people you interact with. Your posture should be upright. Your stride should be strong and proud, oozing confidence with each step. Your style should be measured by your smile, even in the heat of the moment when your normal reaction would be to scowl. Instead, smirk to establish resilience over yourself and others. Swag is permitted! Practice behaving properly. Showing professionalism can result in bringing calmness to a situation where the tension is escalating. Also it helps to build better business relationships for future endeavors.

Book smarts are scholastically preparing one's self with knowledge to gain advantage and outsmart others. Book smarts don't require a person to be a genius or a bookworm. They are simply preparing and arming yourself with knowledge, which is half the battle. Study local and state laws to understand how to maneuver and minimize risks. Street smarts are the skill to adapt to the environment—usually urban or poverty-stricken rural areas—that a person uses to become resourceful in methods of survival. Examples of people who use street smarts include drug dealers, car thieves, loan sharks, pickpockets, burglars, con artists, and hackers. The list is endless!

The logistics for criminal etiquette have been established, and it is time to move to more important matters. Your survival is what I like to call survival of the fittest. Survival of the fittest is a concept that comes from the Darwinian theory of evolution, where organisms that best adapt to their environment thrive. In modern society, a diluted version of this concept refers to the human species' fight for survival against others in their environment. Fighting for survival doesn't necessarily mean the extinction of another human by executing a form of violence. Rather it is how the situation is handled in its entirety. A time will come when your virility will be tested. Through how you handled the situation, that test will confirm how the rest of your public will judge you.

Your overall survival in the eyes of your public primarily depends on two things: mental strength and physical output. Mental strength is the ability to adapt and stand firm on the decisions you have made. If you know something will have a negative outcome and still allow a person to convince you to do it, you are not mentally strong. As the saying goes, "if you stand for nothing, you will fall for anything." When the time comes, you don't want to be that person taking the fall. Stand firm on your decisions. Believe so deep that you could turn your back on God. If you say you are going to do something, then I suggest you do it. If you do not honor your words and actions, you jeopardize your credibility and may be considered weak. Trust is hard earned and can be easily broken. Your word is your bond, so don't break it for anyone.

Physical output is physically protecting a decision that you stand firm upon. It can be something as simple as not giving up a pair of car keys, so a friend doesn't drive home under the influence. Physical output can cause you to take action that could result in fisticuffs to protect a decision that you stand firm upon.

6

CROOK'S MOVEMENT

As a criminal, you should take certain precautions to ensure your safety as well as the safety of those who revolve around your lifestyle. I will provide you with tips and step-by-step plays on how to further your career. Now allow me to show you how a crook should move!

Any seasoned criminal with some form of intellect will not make themselves vulnerable to harm's way, knowing their lifestyle could lead to severe repercussions at any given time. A crook remains anonymous by laying low, living under the radar, and never publicizing themselves. To avoid being pinpointed, the first thing you need to do is create a nickname or alias. I advise against using your government name, as this is the first thing someone gives up or is asked for when investigated. This eliminates paper trails. Also don't take pictures often. A picture is worth a thousand words. One photo alone can be used to narrow in on a person of interest. We have all heard these famous words from detectives pointing at a picture of a suspect: "Do you know who this person is? Tell me where I can find this person."

Stay clear of social media sites, as anyone anywhere in the world can gather intelligence from your profile. If you are a criminal with a social profile, don't be concerned by how many followers you have on your page but by who is following your page. This form of self-worship will only make it easier for personal attacks. Once you become a criminal, delete your profile.

Another form of self-worship is an exhibitionist a person who likes to be in the limelight. This lack of self-worth will inevitably cause you to get set up, because it will become easier to pinpoint your whereabouts and habits. If you feel the need to step out and enjoy yourself, make sure it is outside of your community and away from all business. Also try to blend in. Blending in is the ability to fit in or adapt to your environment. Loud expressions only make you stand out by attracting attention. Examples of being loud are wearing fancy clothes and bright jewelry, driving exotic cars, flashing money, constantly being in the eyes of the public, and always showing off. These are the behaviors that a person should not do if they wish to have a prominent criminal career. Once spotted on someone's radar, it is almost impossible to stay clear of it. To move in silence has dual meanings, as it pertains to speaking and motion.

Speak clear enough to be heard by the listener but low enough for eavesdroppers to not hone in on the conversation. The content of a criminal's conversation should only be heard by the parties involved. One should never talk too much, because words have a way of slipping from the lips, and you know the saying: "Loose lips sink ships." Say only what needs to be said, and do away with extra talk. In this lifestyle, less is more when speaking. Be a criminal of a few words. A person who talks too much subjects themselves to being figured out, and once a person loses their ability to be mysterious, they can be exposed and dealt with accordingly. This gives meaning to the expression "silence is golden."

In the art of war, the surprise of silence can be beautiful, as it reduces one's noise from their movement. This helps to deter a surprise attack or stakeout that could be awaiting your arrival. Noisy movement alerts perpetrators that the person of interest is in range, so practice going and coming without alerting others of your entry or exit. Move like the wind, steady flowing and never taking form. Every day, maneuver as if you were being followed. Stay sharp. Move fast. Always make it hard for anyone to keep up with you. Never be idle for any length of time. If you stop too long, you will expose yourself to being noticed or studied. Take glimpses over your shoulder when in motion. In case you are being watched, constantly change your course of direction to and from your destinations to cause confusion. Get in the habit of observing out-of-place elements in your environment. Double-check when approaching residents, go past and circle the area before returning.

7

THIRST SYNDROME

Thirst syndrome is a craving that causes a person to behave in a self-destructive manner, triggered by an uncontrolled desire to fulfill a lust. It can cause a person to act without thinking about the consequences of their actions during their quest to seek glory—hence the saying "going out in a blaze of glory." Thirst syndrome can breed hate, greed, jealousy, and envy among other vices. You may not be the intended target of a person suffering from thirst syndrome, but their corrupted state of mind could place you in harm's way. It is crucial that you remove these people from your circle. If that's not possible, I suggest you remove yourself. It will only be a matter of time until their stubbornness catches up to you.

In this chapter, I will teach you how to read and be on the alert for these uncanny people of interest. This is merely a poker game, and everyone has a tell. You just need to look closer and know what you are looking for. The universe is constantly giving signals; your job is to be mindful of these signals when they appear. The eyes are the windows to our souls. Eyes are able to direct energy when focused on a particular object. If you look into a person's eyes, you may be surprised by what you discover or feel. Sometimes just standing next to somebody or making eye contact may cause an unexplainable feeling of discomfort, which might be your cue to get away from that person.

Ignorance can be displayed in general conversation in several ways. Interrupting someone while they are talking, always talking, and never listening illustrate a disrespectful and stubborn persona. Negative verbiage usually highlights their ignorance. This can come in the form of phrases such as "I could care less" or "whatever happens just happens" or the most notable, "I don't give a fuck." These phrases are all signals that this person is in a state of indifference and ignorance.

If you are assessing whether or not it is worth investing time and energy into partnerships by weighing the pros and cons, here are a few simple questions to ask yourself that will give you clarity: What can you learn from being around this person? What does this person have to offer? Is there the potential for a strong bond or alliance that will benefit both parties? Early detection of these uncanny characters can eliminate future quarrels or potential rivalries.

In conclusion, we all have a thirst in some shape or form, but some control it more or less than others. If you are powered by positive thoughts and tunnel vision, your thirst can be used as a tool to reach your ultimate goal.

No Honor among Thieves

Honor among thieves is the sentiment that even criminals must have a common code of conduct among one another. No honor among thieves means that criminals cannot be honest or trusted, even by each other. It is the direct dispute of its proverb counterpart.

God created the Ten Commandments for us to live peacefully among one another. The Bible even goes as far as to state an eye for an eye, a tooth for a tooth, and a life for a life. This further confirms that under certain injustices, retribution is reasonable, but if it's not handled properly, it can be detrimental. Scripture also mentions that humanity should create a government and govern their own land. God never declared or decided who got control after the people he appointed passed, yet we all fall under the umbrella of jurisdiction and can be judged in the court of law, even if the opinion is culturally biased.

In this lifestyle you will find that there is no standard of conduct being upheld by your peers, and when that occurs, it may leave you with few options, depending on the depth of the atrocity. Once violated, criminals cannot seek help from a courtroom like regular citizens. They will most likely take different measures and commit more obscure acts for retribution, holding court in the streets.

If someone is detrimental to your self-preservation, one may look for other methods of removal, such as blackmail, bribery, or payoffs. Who is to say that once someone is paid off, they will stay away by any means? If that happens, they may feel they only have a few remaining options. That is not true. This is the point where you put your emotions aside and get creative, enabling your tunnel vision to defeat the opposition.

Control your own fate; you are the ruler of all you survey. Only you know what must be done to secure your future, because only God can judge you, but remember, we all must reap what we sow. Applying bodily harm or the elimination of life should only be an act committed under immediate defense from harm's way.

Imagine if a life were lost out of malice; it would only lead to self-destruction from any attempts to cover up the error. One lie leads to another, and murder only begets more murder, so live righteous, even in a criminal lifestyle. No matter the cost, never risk your freedom or life. These two things are far more priceless. They are why you entered this lifestyle in the first place.

In a duel between rivals, there are two outcomes: the victor and the victim. Know which one you are beforehand, and then make the proper adjustments needed. Victory is far more satisfying when a rival has to live with the repercussions of defeat and cannot return the favor. After all, revenge is a dish best served cold. Make them wish they were dead.

POSITIONS OF POWER

This chapter will strongly focus on constructing and organizing the infrastructure of a gang, crew, mob, pack, firm, click, squad, or team—whichever label you choose to give your organization. Most organizations already have an infrastructure with positions and roles for each member. You know the breakdowns: chiefs, lieutenants, treasurers, enforcers, prospects, or however you rename the slots. There is even street status for successful members. These organizations are made strong and built by the young—mainly boys—who become adults in their culture. Club doors will always be open, and rooms will be filled with new blood eager to be cultivated for a sense of belonging, shelter, or safety.

Children seeking refuge are the easiest to recruit, and once hoodwinked, they can be shaped and molded. When recruiting, the plan is to feed the idle minds of the misguided and install value. Create a belief system for the misguided youth while giving them a place in the organization where society failed them; this will send a signal of reassurance. In doing so, you give the misguided youth a purpose, and in return, you will receive their devotion.

The process after recruiting is initiation, which is standard protocol for would-be members who wish to pledge their allegiance. After the initiation is complete, the organization will test their devotion, how they hold up, and how much they earn for the organization; this is the probation period. Once they are truly a member, they will have to continue putting in work for the organization to stay relevant, move up in rank, and pay dues. The commitment becomes their lives, until it destroys their lives. Some youths are already on the path to destruction without being aware of the lifetime of danger they have subjected themselves to. They will become soldiers in a never-ending war; therefore, the organization should act like a corporate company in America. After all, crime is a business.

In order for the organization to be triumphant in its existence, it must make changes within the company and then go outside the box to complete the changes. Leaders should see themselves as politicians. Even though their intentions for the organization could be completely selfish, they must help the community in order to obtain their hidden agenda—just like politicians.

A true leader should be able to identify the characteristics of the members they employ. Fear and paranoia will lead you to believe that there are members not cut out for this lifestyle and that their initiation is only to seek safety. As I've mentioned before, to ignore that instinct would be foolish. Members that are deemed unfit should not be exiled from the organization because they don't have the commitment or urge to commit crimes or because they prefer reading a book over hitting the punching bag. Instead they should be transformed into tools that will aid the organization in methods other than crime, so the organization can continue to thrive in other aspects or even crossover into legal aspects. There will be members who have the potential to become greater than who they are, but they don't have the push or resources to escape their confines. It is the responsibility of the leader to provide such services. Give them what they need, so you can get what you want. Exploit them for what they are worth. Everything must serve a purpose. Remember, if a person cannot be used, then they are useless.

These members I refer to as tools are sleeper cells whose objectives are to set them on education and career destinations that provide for both parties. The sleeper cells will be more than grateful, because they have a sense of direction but are limited to harm's way. They will work for the system, but their loyalty will remain, not just because they owe it their lives but because it served its purpose.

The only true way to minimize failure and reduce risk against the system is to work from the inside. The system is too well equipped to outsmart and too powerful to take on. There is power in numbers, so if you can't beat them, join them. In doing so, your organization will be given an inside advantage, and knowing is half the battle. All these tools (members) put into place for the organization's benefit increase loyalty, because they have atoned for the support system. Not every member of an organization has to be a full-fledged criminal. They could aid the actual criminals but have limited responsibilities, increasing the safety of the organization and reducing maximum risk.

When fate detonates and finally decides to push that big red button, destroying the existence of the organization, the ultimate goal will have already been accomplished. The infrastructural system will already have members on their life courses because of the direction inside the organization. Even the few who have chosen to play out a life of crime to the fullest will become legends.

10

HOME AIN'T SWEET

Where the criminal lays their head must remain confidential at all times to secure the safety of themselves and others who may live there. Revealing where you live is akin to allowing others access to you whenever they desire. Never make yourself accessible at another person's convenience. You can never really know their intentions with this lifestyle. Making it hard for anyone to locate you at their leisure will help avoid worst-case scenarios. Don't put yourself in harm's way. You won't have to tell someone to get off your property if they don't know where you live. Your location should only be disclosed to those closest to you and or on a need-to-know basis. Business can go bad at any moment, and when trouble strikes, you don't want it to land on your doorstep. Keep business and personal affairs separate. Don't allow them to mix, or a tornado could brew, taking everything you've worked so hard for with it.

Functioning as a member of society can be draining and morally desensitizing. It can be stressful, having to stay sharp 24/7 and never letting your guard down, all the while having the unsettling realization that something could go wrong at any second. Home is important, as it allows the body to reset to its normal functioning levels. When a person enters their domain, they tend to lower their survival defenses in the moments of comfort.

As humans, we are required to eat, sleep, shower, and defecate in order to operate fully, and at these moments, we are exposed literally. Just because a person's physical and mental defenses might slightly decrease, it doesn't mean they can't store the same level of strength in other tools, maintaining that constant defense. There are several tools one can use in the home to protect themselves and loved ones. Canines are great defensive tools when raised in a loving environment, trained, and kept mainly around family. They will instinctively deter strange intruders who try to enter the grounds. Pay attention to warning signs; raise your awareness in your household. Be on the lookout for the unusual. Set parameters that lock tight and are durable, such as gates, fences, and doors. Alarms and security cameras are your eyes and ears while you lay idle. Firearms and weapons should be stationed throughout the house and easily accessible. Have an escape route in your home, just in case.

Powerful defenses have layers that must be chipped away before their cores can be infiltrated. Intruders should have to literally hurdle obstacles before attempting to reach their intended target—you. By adding layers to your defense, you make it hard for them from the onset.

You can change the intruder's course, and several things could happen. They could retreat from fatigue. Their time could be wasted from the hassle. There could be a delay in their movement speed. All of which allows you ample time to ready yourself for immediate action, providing you with that offensive dynamo's edge. For every good offense is a great defense, and defense wins games.

11

INITIATE EXIT PLAN

As mentioned previously, it is impossible for a person immersed in this particular lifestyle to flourish and grow to their full potential, because any attempt would be futile or foolish. Set an ultimate goal for yourself. If you achieve it, salute yourself. Disengage from all activities if the goal isn't met due to the risk of extending beyond further levels, if you obtain sufficient capital or resources to manage for a period of time. We will work on beginning your new lifestyle with the assets you have acquired, making your transition from the under accomplished to an accomplished member of society.

Wealth is not just acquiring and having an abundance of resources but a state of mind. It is a form of happiness derived from being content and appreciative of what you have. That being said, this is your transition into completing your ultimate goal, creating a new lifestyle, and becoming the person you were meant to be.

I will help you by using the assets you acquired to break your current life patterns, which have kept you stagnant.

So how does a person make the transition from an illegal lifestyle to a legal one without having a firm grasp on what they actually want to accomplish? The answer is quite simple, unless your objective requires too much time or money to break the barrier. If you decide to challenge the issue and force your way through this barrier, you are striving against strife, and I salute you. A person may have multiple talents, skills, and trades that have not come to fruition, because they have yet to be recognized or lack motivation. First, you must find what it is you enjoy doing in life or are naturally good at, besides criminal activity. The assets you acquired will serve as tools of mediation to ease the frustrations that once impaired your judgment but now allow you to operate with a clear mind, enabling deep concentration to reflect on your inner self, capabilities, and future goals. No one can operate clearly when they are overwhelmed by stress.

Once you have come to the realization of what strikes your fancy or what you are comfortable doing, the next step is learning how to extract the good from the bad. This is why I am a staunch believer that everything has a purpose. Springing from your lifestyle, habits, and hobbies, an opportunity lies, just waiting to be discovered. It doesn't matter if you are diagnosed with OCD and can't pass a dirty room without having the urge to clean it; from my perspective, you are an organized perfectionist. This skill serves a purpose. You become marketable, and that is your business right there. If you are a nymphomaniac whose fetish is voyeurism, the adult film business is a possible field that you could venture into; therefore, you are marketable.

Start-ups are not complicated. It comes by way of three categories: DIY, online services or hiring a business professional. Whichever direction you choose, it shouldn't cost much time but you must spend money to make money.

Once the business is up and running, make a mental reminder that nothing comes without hard work. Maintaining the business once it's thriving will rely entirely on having tunnel vision and the determination to see it through successfully. It is not considered work if you enjoy what you do! It will soon become apparent to many of you that not everyone is meant to be an entrepreneur, mogul, or power broker. Some will have to settle for more traditional lifestyles, jobs, houses, cars, partners, or pets.

Occupationally look for something you enjoy, if not something you are skilled in. This will make for a more-tolerable working condition. You don't have to rush anything; you have ample time. The ultimate goal for your previous earnings is to financially back yourself until you choose your occupation. But spend wisely. Choose a vehicle you can afford. Avoid expensive purchases, as they draw unneeded attention and shorten your assets, which should be used as a lifeline for maintaining your survival. Date freely until the right person appears.

Once you have acquired a decent occupation that you can endure and start to accumulate a solid paper trail, you may choose to establish a line of credit. If you decide to open a bank account for future endeavors, never put all your eggs in one basket. You may have become an honest patron of society, but never stop thinking like a crook. You can tender a fair amount into the bank, but there is nothing wrong with that shoebox or under-the-mattress money in case of emergencies. A decent occupation will keep you from having to use your previous earnings apart from extreme circumstances. Read chapter 3 again, and incorporate it into your new lifestyle.

EPILOGUE

Believe it or not, crime is real and operates as a conduit to bring about change or fulfillment to a lifestyle, justifying its existence. Criminal or not, everyone deserves the chance to become a normal member of society. Although the concept behind *The Unconstitutional and Unwritten Laws of Crime* may cross the immorality line, its entirety was written for the greater good— to evolve readers who chose to become criminal participants by educating and making them subconsciously aware of how to form beneficial habits. A touch of skill to normal protocol can be the action that prevents downfall. I feel guiding the participants' aides as a deterrent, lowering the unnecessary ills that spawn from crime, such as theft, violence, double crosses, murder, and revenge. In return, this affects everyone.

There are criminals who feel they don't have any other choices due to lack of support, education, or financial backing. Whatever the circumstances may be, the government targets certain populations, mainly based on ethnicity and social class. My goal is to break that cycle before they lock you up and throw away the key. At that point, your life is no longer your own, and you become federal or state property. Correctional institutions receive enormous capital through government funding for housing prisoners. Inmates are paid way below minimum wage while companies use their labor for cents an hour, decreasing their labor cost and saving millions. This isn't fair and is a crime. Rehabilitating criminals is the least of the government's concerns.

Lowering the crime rate will reduce the need for bigoted, racist, and corrupt police officers, lawyers (including district attorneys), judges, and correction officers in positions of power. It will help lay them off. Unused labor at the government's expense will most likely lead to downsizing and reduced funding. If the current crime rate miraculously declined, these people would probably be out of work, and the good few would just be casualties of the unemployment line. The money distributed to local and state governments for budgets could then be targeted and diversified to more important objectives, such as health care, education, and public assistance.

Crime is necessary but should not be glorified, because unfortunately it is an epidemic that can affect everyone. For example, an illegal deal could go terribly wrong because one participant tried to double-cross the other, which would spill out violently in return, disturbing the peace, jeopardizing innocent bystanders, and subjecting everyone to harm's way.

Sentences given to first offenders usually don't meet the stature of the crime, depending on the charge; if it was not committed out of malice, they should be given a fair chance. The charges are far too harsh when the people are just trying to make something of themselves. Thirty-year sentences for drug trafficking on a first offense is literally a fraction of their natural life for a person in their early twenties. That is outrageous.

I personally feel that commonwealth law should be abolished. Serving a sentence should be harsh. How will a person learn if the punishment is scarce? Spare the rod, spoil the child. But the punishment should not be unforgiving. I believe that criminals convicted of a crime should be incarcerated with shackled hands and feet and have their fingers worked to the bones while they rebuild the community they once took from. The majority of those who carry out the laws cannot relate to poverty-stricken people in rural or urban areas. The powers that be who create these laws don't have consciences for lives they don't know, lifestyles they are not familiar with, or people they can't relate to.

Crime will never stop, because it is a necessary evil. It is like traveling through evil in order to get to the good. Crime will continuously evolve economically and through the ages, bringing forth more skilled and less compassionate human beings, because error plagues our generations. The Bible states that the sins of a father will be revisited in the son. If a person dies or gets incarcerated because they lived a life of crime, their offspring will most likely be subject to a similar fate. Why is that? I don't know, but I have some ideas. Why are offspring so similar to their ancestors? History repeats itself. The offspring will spawn from where their makers left, wearing their marks (facial features, attitude, last name, domain, etc.). The absence of would-be parental advisors limits guidance, causing the offspring to develop their own sense of survival from their makers' prior conditions.

Legal guardians are not the same as biological parents. The connection of a bloodline is missing, and that offspring will always feel like an outcast deep down, even with love. Grandparents will face hardships trying to keep up with the offspring's youthfulness, and one parent is not enough to raise a child. Like they say, it takes a village. But those were the old days. Now there are no villages. That offspring is on their own once their immediate family has been broken.

If you are not that offspring's parents but care for the youth, I advise you not to discipline or reprimand them without factoring in that too much discipline can cause them to rebel. If they are big enough and old enough to rebel, they will; therefore, confronting the misguided directly is strongly not suggested in certain cases. What you can do is hone in on their skills and play to their interests without overstepping your boundary. The offspring will appreciate you more for not forcing their hand. Regardless of what you may think, that misguided offspring is going to do what they best know how to do to survive or feel better about themselves. Your hidden agenda is to manipulate them through the direction of interests, which will cause them to make a positive transformation without being aware of the transition.

Costantino D'Amato was the boxer manager and trainer who founded professional boxer Mike Tyson. It was under D'Amato's tutelage that Tyson became the youngest heavyweight boxer to win a world title. Tyson was a young, troubled teen with a poor upbringing and was always in and out of trouble. It was D'Amato who took notice of Tyson's rebellious and aggressive style and decided to convert a would-be thug into a professional boxer. Tyson himself admitted that if it weren't for meeting D'Amato, he would have been in jail or possibly dead within a few. Good thing he was redirected to a positive outcome. Tyson said he owes everything to D'Amato. Today, Tyson is a family man, boxer promoter and manager, book writer, and actor. He is also one of my few heroes because of his evolution. This is a perfect example of the transformation of potential energy into kinetic energy. The misguided youth just need support systems to keep them from falling as well as a slight push every now and then to keep them from going in the wrong direction.

About the Book

The Unwritten and Unconstitutional Laws of Crime is a strategic guide or bible for how to not only function but thrive in a life of crime. It is a fusion of criminology and philosophy consisting of planned preparation, tried methods from experience, and research to increase longevity. This book is a step-by-step tutorial that specializes in the entry into and exit from this lifestyle. No life of crime goes without hardships, but I have composed a book that shows how to minimize the effects. This book is a quick read with a no-holds-barred, direct approach. It was written not for entertainment purposes but strictly for the purposes of deterring the reader from crime and educating those who chose to participate in this lifestyle.

Printed in the United States
by Baker & Taylor Publisher Services

Printed in the United States
by Baker & Taylor Publisher Services